HAWAII

Waikiki Beach, one of the most celebrated in the world, was once a swamp; now its hotels and apartment houses, shops, theaters and restaurants would be difficult to count. (On the preceding page is shown the Royal Coat of Arms of Hawaii.)

HAWAII

by **GORDON SAGER**

with an introduction by
SENATOR DANIEL K. INOUYE

 KODANSHA INTERNATIONAL LTD.
TOKYO, NEW YORK & SAN FRANCISCO

Photography by Bon Color, Don Watnick, Ichiro Nakagawa, Izuo Ishii, Masumi Hamada (Kodansha Photolab), Orion Press, Rainbow Photo, Yoshikazu Shirakawa.

Distributors:
UNITED STATES: *Kodansha International/USA, Ltd., through Harper & Row, Publishers, Inc., 10 East 53rd Street, New York, New York 10022.* SOUTH AMERICA: *Harper & Row, International Department.* CANADA: *Fitzhenry & Whiteside Limited, 150 Lesmill Road, Don Mills, Ontario.* MEXICO AND CENTRAL AMERICA: *HARLA S. A. de C. V., Apartado 30-546, Mexico 4, D. F.* UNITED KINGDOM: *TABS, 7 Maiden Lane, London WC2.* EUROPE: *Boxerbooks Inc., Limmatstrasse 111, 8031 Zurich.* AUSTRALIA AND NEW ZEALAND: *Book Wise (Australia) Pty. Ltd., 104–8 Sussex Street, Sydney.* THAILAND: *Central Department Store Ltd., 306 Silom Road, Bangkok.* HONG KONG AND SINGAPORE: *Books for Asia Ltd., 30 Tat Chee Avenue, Kowloon; 65 Crescent Road, Singapore 15.* THE FAR EAST: *Japan Publications Trading Company, P.O. Box 5030, Tokyo International, Tokyo.*

Published by Kodansha International Ltd., 2–12–21 Otowa, Bunkyo-ku, Tokyo 112 and Kodansha International/USA, Ltd., 10 East 53rd Street, New York, New York 10022 and 44 Montgomery Street, San Francisco, California 94104. Copyright in Japan 1969 by Kodansha International Ltd. All rights reserved. Printed in Japan.

LCC 69–16369
ISBN 0-87011-072-1
JBC 0325-780838-2361

First edition, 1969
Seventh printing, 1976

Contents

Introduction

HAWAII remains a land of thrusting tropical volcanic peaks whose sides rush down to multi-hued sandy beaches and into the blue-green seas which have caressed the island chain since the first volcanoes roared into earthly prominence far out in the Pacific.

But Hawaii is much more than a temporary oasis where man can refresh his spirit and physical well-being. It is the permanent home of a people whose destiny is still to be fulfilled. It is the haven for a multi-racial society whose mores contain the seed of hope for all mankind.

Those of us who are blessed with the opportunity to live in these islands believe we can help to build a better world for our fellow men by setting an example for all who visit our shores.

We practice the spirit of Aloha—of love of our fellow human beings—and find contentment with one another. We pray that the many thousands who visit us each year will carry this spirit back to their homes and that they, too, will find the inner peace which we cherish so much.

DANIEL K. INOUYE
United States Senator

HAWAII

The First Aloha State

"IN THE morning of the 18th, an island made its appearance, bearing northeast by east; and soon after we saw more land bearing north and entirely detached from the former. Both had the appearance of being high land. . . .

"At this time, we were in some doubt whether or no the land before us was inhabited; but this doubt was soon cleared up by seeing some canoes coming off the shore toward the ships. I immediately brought to, to give them time to join us. . . ."

And thus an English gentleman of the eighteenth century was suddenly catapulted—as though in a time-capsule—all the way back to the Stone Age. The date was January 18th, 1778; the writer was Captain James Cook; and the islands he had just "discovered" were those of the Hawaiian archipelago, volcanic peaks of a submerged mountain range, that had been "discovered" at least ten centuries earlier by quite a different people altogether.

They "were of a brown color," wrote Captain Cook, "and though of the common size were stoutly made. There was little difference in the cast of their color but a considerable variation in their features, some of their visages not being very unlike those of Europeans. The hair of most of them was cropped pretty short;

7

others had it flowing loose; and with a few, it was tied in a bunch on the crown of the head. In all, it seemed to be naturally black; but most of them had stained it, as is the practice of the Friendly Islanders, with some stuff which gave it a brown or burnt color. In general they wore beards.

"They had no ornaments about their persons, nor did we observe that their ears were perforated; but some were punctured on the hands or near the groin, though in a small degree; and the bits of cloth which they wore were curiously stained with red, black, and white colors. They seemed very mild and had no arms of any kind, if we except some small stones which they had evidently brought for their own defense; and these they threw overboard when they found that they were not wanted."

These were Polynesians, probably from around Tahiti, who had brought with them some gods and some customs that the Europeans (and the Americans) were to find distinctly unattractive, or even downright horrible, but at the same time they had brought one other custom that was to prove immensely useful to the adventuring Westerners—and perhaps to the "native" Hawaiians as well. The word for this custom, which still survives, is *aloha,* and it means—among other things—a friendly greeting. "The very instant I leapt on shore," wrote the Captain, "the collected body of the natives fell flat upon their faces and remained in that very humble posture till by expressive signs I prevailed upon them to rise. They then brought a great many small pigs, which they presented to me, with plantain trees, using much the same ceremonies that we had seen practiced on such occasions at the Society and other islands; and a long prayer being spoken by a single person, in which others of the assembly sometimes joined, I expressed my acceptance of their proffered friendship by giving them in return such presents as I had brought with me from the ship for that purpose. . . ."

But the meeting between Captain Cook and the Hawaiians did not end as happily as it began—for in addition to their agreeable *aloha* habit, which made them ritually hospitable to strangers, these descendants of Stone Age Polynesians preserved their belief in both *mana* and *kapu*. The former referred to a supernatural power that could be possessed by people as well as by objects. A king who was particularly rich in *mana* could be a source of great benefit to his people, as well as of great danger. For that reason the system of *kapu*—or *tapu* or *tabu*, as it is called by other Polynesians —was initiated, and for infractions of many prohibitions the punishment was death. The bestowers of *mana* were the gods, of whom the Hawaiians worshiped hundreds, although special reverence was paid to Kane, creator of all life; to Kaneloa, who ruled the land of the dead; to Ku, the god of war; and to Lono, the god of peace and the harvest. Captain Cook, possessing those two great ships, the *Resolution* and the *Discovery*, plus the miracle of iron, was declared to be a reincarnation of Lono. Like the Aztecs, the Hawaiians had a legend about a white god from the sea; and like Cortez, Cook benefited from it—for a time.

Above all, the Hawaiians wanted iron for their fish-hooks, and in return for a nail or two would give Captain Cook an entire day's provision for the crews of both his ships. He named the islands after the Earl of Sandwich, First Lord of the Admiralty, and was appreciative of the islanders' kindness and grace, solicitous after their health, and respectful of their sailing ability. For they had, after all, at a time when most sailors in the world seldom ventured beyond sight of a coastline, crossed thousands of miles of the in-

1. *Surfing*, one of Hawaii's most ▶
popular sports, is a difficult art to
master—but Hawaiian beachboys do
their best for the tourists.

HAWAII ✻

aptly-named Pacific, guiding themselves largely by the stars but
using also that wide store of knowledge that people who live in
direct communion with nature inevitably acquire.

Their social organization was fairly rigid and probably had
changed very little in the hundreds of years of their occupation
of the islands. At the top were the hereditary chiefs, or *alii*, with
their attendants, courtiers, seers, doctors, and the like. The mass
of the people were fishermen and farmers, who supported their
rulers by paying taxes in the form of produce of various kinds as
well as the all-important tapa cloth, which was woven by the women
out of the inner bark of the mulberry tree. Men did all the cooking
—and most of the desirable foods were tabu for women.

This is the land that Captain Cook discovered for the West and
that he left, after a two-weeks' stay, in order to try to find the
Northwest Passage. It was on his return, the following November,
that he was at first deified, then robbed (for iron), and in the ensuing
disorders killed. After death, however, his bones, stripped of their
flesh, were claimed by the chiefs as sacred relics; some of the Captain's bones, covered with red feathers, which were also sacred,
were placed in a temple to be worshiped.

This was the land that Captain Cook discovered and these were
the people whom American missionaries were soon to christianize
in what has been termed the most successful instance of mass
conversion in Christian history. Certainly it was a success from the
proselytizers' point of view. But first, events of national importance
were to pave the way for the conquering missionaries.

Some twenty years before Captain Cook's arrival, some twenty
years before tea was dumped into Boston Harbor, a pregnant woman
fled to Waipio Valley, in the mountains of Kohala, on the island of

2. *Hula,* sacred dance of the original Polynesian settlers, was banned by the missionaries and revitalized by King Kalakaua.

3. *Silver Sword,* with its pointed silvery leaves, is found both in Hawaii —and the Himalayas. In Hawaii it flowers in August.

❦ THE FIRST ALOHA STATE

Hawaii, to escape King Alapai, who had determined—so story says—to put her unborn child to death because a seer had foretold that he would become a killer of kings and monarch of all the islands. Lightning and thunder accompanied the birth of the boy, the heavens opened, deluging the islands with rain, and there was also a comet seen—Halley's, perhaps. Despite King Alapai, the boy lived, to become King Kamehameha I, the unifier of Hawaii —which, two hundred years after his birth, was to be voted the fiftieth of the United States.

While Captain Cook was in Hawaii, Kamehameha went aboard the English vessels, and there he realized that to withstand the white man's power Hawaii would need to make use of the white man's magic—and to be unified. After conquering the islands of Hawaii, Maui, and Molokai, he was about to attack Oahu when its king, an old man, asked him to wait till he, the old king, was dead. Presumably Kamehameha agreed, for it was not until four years later that he sailed to Oahu with a thousand canoes and two four-pounders manned by British castaways whom he had enlisted. He overcame the resistance of the old king's son and then succeeded in persuading the island of Kauai to join his United Kingdom without recourse to force. He was now monarch of all the islands.

He proved to be as skillful in the arts of peace as in those of war. Captain Otto von Kotzebue, a German who served in the czar's navy and who was very much at home in the Pacific, said of him: "He is a man of great wisdom. Giving his people only things he considers useful, he tries to increase the *happiness*, not the *wants*, of his people." The king was also an extremely shrewd trader who was more than willing to cooperate with the foreigners in the national interest—but who refused to be cheated. As soon as he dis-

15

covered that merchants were supplying goods that were not according to specification, he refused any longer to deal with them. He himself, though a good bargainer, was absolutely scrupulous in business matters.

Skilled foreign laborers were encouraged to settle in the islands, and in this way many of Kamehameha's subjects became skilled laborers too. He sold the sandalwood monopoly to American merchants, who transported the fragrant wood to China, where it was in great demand. At last he bought a brig himself—which he named after his favorite wife—and when upon its first voyage to China, it showed a substantial profit, he promptly began buying more and soon had over forty merchant vessels in his fleet.

All foreigners who were privileged to speak to him were deeply impressed by his stature as a great human being as well as by his overpowering physical presence. He was extremely gracious to both Otto von Kotzebue and George Vancouver, the famous British explorer. To von Kotzebue he said one day, as he was showing him the sacred images of the gods, "These are our Gods, whom I worship. Whether I do right or wrong I do not know, but I follow my faith, which cannot be wicked, as it commands me never to do ill." He permitted his favorite wife, Kaahumanu, to meet Vancouver, who remarked afterwards that she is "the most beautiful woman in the South Seas."

She was also one of the most progressive. When Kamehameha died in 1819, his bones—according to ancient custom—were hidden secretly away in a cave, and his son Liholiho ascended the throne, taking the title of Kamehameha II. The "favorite wife," Kaahumanu, was to be co-ruler, as a kind of prime minister—but she soon became the country's real ruler, and it was she, along with the young king's mother, who inspired him to decree first the abolition of idol-worship, then second the end of food-tabus. Women were now free to eat with men, and to eat the same foods that men ate. Hawaii's ancient religion had suddenly died.

It was into this spiritual vacuum that the Reverend Hiram Bingham and the Reverend Asa Thurston brought their "First Company" of Congregationalists to the islands in March, 1820: the first company of that army of Christian soldiers from New England and New York who, under the influence of Jonathan Edwards, were to evangelize the pagan Hawaiians so thoroughly that Mark Twain, when he visited the islands some forty years later, was moved to remark: "They all belong to the church and are fonder of theology than they are of pie; they will sweat out a sermon as long as the Declaration of Independence; the duller it is the more it infatuates them."

The spiritual climate of New England was a propitious one for this remarkable accomplishment. Having heard Jonathan Edwards preach the Great Awakening, the people of New England—of Connecticut especially—had accepted the doctrine that the only thing worth striving for in life was divine redemption. The hope of "salvation" was the mainspring of all action, and to carry that hope to the "heathen" was considered one of the most splendid things any man could do with his life. The youth of New England— Yale students in particular—were fired with enthusiasm by the idea of bringing salvation to lost souls, and the American Board of Commissioners for Foreign Missions was accordingly formed to channelize this zeal. Young men and women were ready to go anywhere on earth that God called them.

The call to the Hawaiian islands was made more urgent by the

17

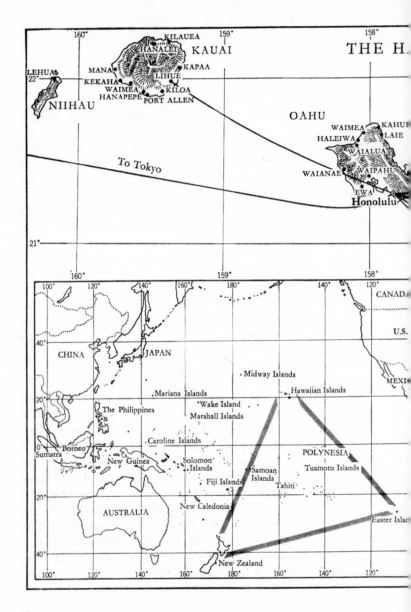

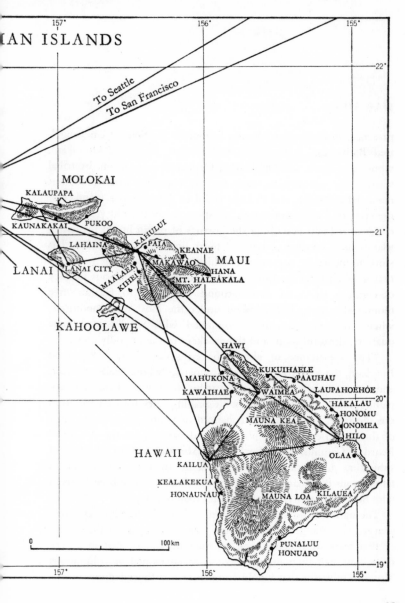

To Seattle
To San Francisco

MOLOKAI
KALAUPAPA
KAUNAKAKAI   PUKOO
LAHAINA   KAHULUI
KEANAE
LANAI   LANAI CITY   PAIA
MAKAWAO   MAUI
MAALAEA   HANA
KIHEI   MT. HALEAKALA

KAHOOLAWE

HAWI
KUKUIHAELE
MAHUKONA   PAAUHAU
KAWAIHAE   WAIMEA   LAUPAHOEHOE
HAKALAU
HONOMU
MAUNA KEA   ONOMEA
HILO
HAWAII
KAILUA   OLAA
KEALAKEKUA
HONAUNAU
MAUNA LOA   KILAUEA

0   100 km

PUNALUU
HONUAPO

presence, at the Foreign Mission School for the Sons of Unevangel-
ized Barbarians, in Cornwall, Connecticut, of Henry Obookiah,
whose real name was Opukahaia. Orphaned early in life by tribal
warfare, he was sent to study for the Hawaiian priesthood, but
managed to escape, and in 1810 sailed to America as a member of
the crew of a merchant vessel. He spent the next eight years being
christianized and describing the horrors of pagan life in his native
islands until he died of typhoid fever on February 19, 1818. His
story immediately became the subject of a best-selling pamphlet
that inspired the First Company to undertake the hideous journey
of eighteen thousand miles around the Horn to Hawaii—five
months aboard the brig *Thaddeus* under the most dire conditions,
where constant seasickness combined with wholly inadequate
quarters, dreadful food, and the mockery of the ungodly crew.

"The appearance of almost naked savages," said Reverend
Bingham, the leader of the First Company, "whose heads and feet,
and much of their sunburned, swarthy skins, were bare, was appalling. Some of our number, with gushing tears, turned away from
the spectacle." The number consisted of young newlyweds, most
of them married in haste just before departure, for the American
Board of Commissioners for Foreign Missions had no intention of
subjecting unmarried divinity students to the easy Hawaiian
temptations the Board had heard so much about. The Board agreed
with St. Paul that marriage was better than burning.

The natives who swarmed down to greet the *Thaddeus* as it dis-
charged its strange cargo had no idea how appalling they were,
or that tears were being shed on their behalf—or that in a very
short time half their number would be enveloped in voluminous
Mother Hubbards that would completely veil those famous volup-

tuous curves from concupiscent male eyes. To clothe that naked female flesh was one of the first injunctions laid on the lady missionaries by their leader. It was not an easy task. Female chiefs weighed, so it was said, in the neighborhood of three hundred pounds.

But before the urgent business of clothing the savage could be attempted, the missionaries first required permission to remain in the islands—and this permission Liholiho was reluctant to grant. Perhaps he feared that the new religion the missionaries had come to preach would upset the status quo, a thing no monarch likes to see happen—or perhaps he feared that it would deprive him of some of his five well-padded wives. In any case, he procrastinated. It was only after twelve days of uncertainty that he finally agreed to let the Americans stay for a year; he gave them places to live and servants to work for them. His co-ruler, Queen Kaahumanu, was no more enthusiastic than he about the arrival of the evangelists, but she agreed that the risk of a year's trial was worth running.

"If we would see the Gospel take effect on a nation," said Bingham, "its light must be diffused over the whole nation. The mass must have opportunity to see it simultaneously. Christianity should be made by precept and example to radiate from many different points so extensively that all the tribes may have the means of judging its merits." And that is precisely what happened. The missionaries seemed to have the miraculous power to multiply themselves geometrically, and they endured the hardships of their first years on the islands with more than Christian fortitude. Flea-ridden grass huts were not what the young ladies of Connecticut had been accustomed to.

This confrontation between a fanatic band of Christians (soon followed by other bands, equally fanatic) and the naked "savages"

HAWAII 〼

of Hawaii is one of the strangest in history—and its outcome is not altogether easy to account for. Perhaps one of the most compelling reasons for the success of the missionaries is the fact that the Hawaiians had just been deprived of their ancient religion. In persuading King Kamehameha II to promulgate his reforms, the dowager queens had upset the pineapple-cart more violently than they anticipated. The more primitive the people, the more reassurance they seem to require that the supernatural is not antipathetic—and this reassurance the zealous Christian missionaries were able to supply to a people recently bereft of it.

There is, of course, the further fact that the Christians preached the doctrine that *all* men may find salvation. And this doctrine must have had its attractions for a people who had hitherto lived their lives in the belief that only the chiefs possessed *mana* and so must be implicitly obeyed. The fact remains, however, that the king, the royal family, and the chiefs were the first of the missionaries' pupils. Perhaps, like the sophisticated folk in Cavafy's poem, "Waiting for the Barbarians," these grand Hawaiians were merely bored—and so welcomed any diversion, even if it consisted of an hour-long sermon.

Whatever the reason, events now moved swiftly. Within a decade of Bingham's arrival, fifty thousand islanders were being instructed in the Congregationalist faith. The old idols had been toppled over—literally as well as figuratively—and the old dances forbidden, for the hula was, in its origin, a sacred dance. Schools and churches were established; the people were taught to read and write as well as to pray; they were given a written language, into which were translated the Bible and *Pilgrim's Progress*, to help in the salvation of their souls.

The chief opposition to the missionaries came from the other foreign residents—merchants who saw their influence with the chiefs waning, and sailors who found the kind of rest and relaxation they wanted increasingly hard to get. This opposition was to blossom, before too long, into a full-scale war.

Meanwhile, tragedy struck the royal house. Perhaps bored by his Christian instruction, perhaps annoyed at the autocratic tactics of his "prime minister," Dowager Queen Kaahumanu, King Liholiho Kamehameha decided to make a trip to England. He took with him his favorite wife, Kamamalu, and a fairly substantial retinue, arriving in London in May, 1824, where the King and Queen became immediate favorites with society. Before a meeting with King George could take place, however, the Queen was stricken with measles, which proved fatal, and within a week the King was also dead. Their bodies were returned in state to Hawaii aboard *HMS Blonde*, which was commanded by Lord Byron, the poet's cousin.

Liholiho was succeeded on the throne by another son of the first Kamehameha, a boy who had attended the Chiefs' Children's School, under the direction of two American missionaries, Amos Cooke and his wife. The boy was called away to take up his royal duties at the age of twelve. Dowager Queen Kaahumanu acted as Regent until her death in 1832.

King Kamehameha III was a gentle, kindly soul, ill-fitted to stand up against the various pressures, both at home and abroad, that kept building up during his long, thirty-year reign. One, of course, was the enmity between the missionaries and the other white residents as well as with missionaries of other faiths. The Congregationalists wanted Hawaii to be what Connecticut had

23

been, a state with an established religion—and to a large extent they succeeded. Blue Laws were strictly enforced. The only movement to be observed on Sunday was that toward church. All shops or places of amusement were shut. Merchants were annoyed; sailors were infuriated.

Indeed, there was a pitched battle between the crew of the *USS Dolphin* on one side and Reverend Hiram Bingham and his Hawaiian converts on the other. The prize was the prostitutes the sailors fervently believed were their due. They won. "After a visit of three months," wrote Bingham, "the *Dolphin* sailed, having obtained the proud name of 'the mischief-making man-of-war.' With that term was associated the shout of the vile which was heard in the harbor as the first boatload of vile women was seen to pass under its flag. . . ."

Bingham was not a man who perceived shades of gray. "Committing ourselves to the care and protection of our ever-watchful Heavenly Father," he wrote, on the arrival of his company, "and putting ourselves in the power of strangers and pagans, untutored and destitute of the feeling of moral responsibility, intemperate, lewd and thievish, as they were, we unhesitatingly entered into this new mode of life, and as missionary pilgrims, cheerfully took up our abode in that dark, ruined land, which we looked upon as the place of our sojourn and toil while on earth, and the resting place of our bones when our brief pilgrimage should end." Not all white men looked upon Hawaii in quite the same terms, nor did they see it as dark and ruined—although many felt that it was *being* ruined, and being ruined by the missionaries themselves.

"They have been wrong," said the British Consul-General in Honolulu, "in their hot-house plan of forcing Christianity on an unprepared people, endeavoring to make them run before they could walk or even stand alone. . . . They have been wrong in using their great influence with the native government in urging a hard repressive system of legislation. They have been wrong—at least they have been unfortunate—in the personal qualifications of many of their teachers for their task, when so much of a missionary's success depends upon appearance, manner and knowledge."

One of the pieces of legislation they effected was the promulgation of a Bill of Rights and the creation of a legislative body, both of which they persuaded King Kamehameha III to proclaim in 1839—with the result that within a few years several important political positions were held by ex-missionaries. Seven years later, in 1846, at the insistence of the King's missionary advisers, came the most momentous act of his reign—the Great Mahele, or division of lands, by which, after keeping nearly a million acres of land for himself, he parceled out the remainder to the government, the chiefs, and the people. It was intended to be a kind of "emancipation proclamation," allowing everyone in the country to own his own plot of land—but it did not work out quite the way it was intended.

For at the same time, the King annulled the prohibition against foreigners' owning land. The whole concept of the "ownership" of land was vague in the Hawaiian mind. It was the King who had hitherto "owned" Hawaii. People who could file claims simply didn't bother to, and people who did file claims soon found that they were so in debt to wily white traders that the only solution was to hand over what they owned. Good agricultural land sold for around fifty cents an acre.

The missionaries were not backward about acquiring this land, any more than the other white residents, and many of the vast

HAWAII 🌿

Hawaiian fortunes may be said to have started as a result of these two so-called reforms instigated largely by the missionaries themselves. Sons of missionaries went into business, at which they were no less successful than their fathers had been at evangelizing. Native Hawaiians, meanwhile, were still toiling over their books—the Bible and *Pilgrim's Progress*—and dying of white men's diseases.

Of the Mahele, an Hawaiian historian wrote: "Ownership of the land by the King was the rock that formed the anchor of our safety. Now the rock has been shattered by the storm."

Another storm was raging around King Kamehameha III—the obvious desire, from time to time, of England, France, and the United States to annex the islands. At one point, in fact, a British naval officer occupied Hawaii for five months; when his kingdom was restored to him, Kamehameha said, "*Ua mau ke ea o ka 'aina i ka pono*"—"The life of the land is perpetuated in righteousness," which became the motto of Hawaii. After this episode, Hawaiian independence was recognized by the rulers of the three powers, although sporadic threats against it continued to be made, chiefly by the French, threats that Washington viewed with obvious disfavor. There was considerable agitation for outright annexation by America at the time of Kamehameha's death in 1854. He was forty-one years old.

America's interest in Hawaii at that time was, of course, an economic one, centering around two thriving industries: whaling and sugar. (James D. Dole had not yet canned his first pineapple; that momentous event was not to occur until the beginning of the next century.) Sugar exports totaled around five hundred tons a year at the time of the King's death, but it was by no means the booming industry it was destined to become.

Whaling, however, was at its peak and continued so till around 1860, when Edwin L. Drake struck oil at Titusville, Pennsylvania, and the value of whale oil progressively declined in the world's markets. But in 1846 nearly six hundred vessels, with crews totaling some twenty thousand, used the Hawaiian Islands as their headquarters. Honolulu, with its protected harbor and extensive facilities, was the chief port for whalers—but it was also the most expensive, so many captains preferred to go elsewhere. Lahaina was almost as popular as Honolulu, with Koloa and Hilo following close behind.

Whaling-crews were not famous for their respect for law and order: the work was extremely dangerous, while life aboard ship tended to brutalize and demoralize; the men were away from home for years at a stretch, and they were well-paid. The combination, when the crews put in to Hawaiian ports, resulted in a situation the missionaries found deplorable. Others, however, from prostitutes to the royal treasurer, did less deploring. "Native girls," said one of the missionaries, "flock here in the ship season from other parts to get the ready wages of sin." But of course it was not only the girls. "The populace of both sexes," he continued, "were out to get what was a-going. . . ."

The fact that a whaler could base in Hawaii en route to the Yellow Sea or the Sea of Japan and then again six months later en route to South America permitted the ship, with its crew, to remain away from home for much longer periods of time and so make more money for its owners. Thus, the business of supplying and repairing the ships in Hawaii became an extremely lucrative one. To cater to the needs of twenty thousand men on arduous six-month voyages in icy seas taxed the ingenuity of the planters, who were willing to try any crop they thought might thrive in Hawaii and also satisfy the appetites of the whaling men. The Irish potato, imported from New England, made its growers a lot of money. Salt and sugar were required by the ships, cattle and pigs, firewood to try out the oil from the blubber—there was no end to the needs of the sailors, and no end apparently to the ready money captains had at their disposal.

Whaling was a vastly profitable, if speculative, trade. If a whaler was lucky enough to fill its barrels at a time when oil was high on the market, then everyone made a handsome profit—including, of course, the men themselves, for they were paid a share of the profits. Once the price for oil and bone was fixed, usually by the American consul at Honolulu, the owners took their share and then what remained was divided up among the men.

And then the missionaries wrung their hands and prayed for the continued salvation of their converts—while the rest of Hawaii, one way or another, dipped its hands into the sailors' pockets. Shops, taverns, and dance-halls were only the beginning; there were also the importers and traders who supplied them and the girls who filled them; there were tax-collectors and revenue agents; there was the government of Honolulu, which exacted fines for misbehavior—such as five dollars for fornication, thirty dollars for adultery, and fifty dollars for rape. The fine for "desecrating the Sabbath for the first time" was six dollars; for the second time it was twelve dollars; and the fine was "doubled for every repetition." So presumably it cost very little more to commit rape than to desecrate the Sabbath four times: an open invitation, surely, to those of an ungentle nature.

By the time the whaling industry had begun its decline, the sugar industry was on its way toward a boom. Sugar was as old in the islands as the people themselves, for the Polynesians brought cane cuttings among their treasures when they first came—a dwarf variety that soon grew outside every Hawaiian household and that everyone chewed raw. No cane was ground till early in the nineteenth century, when a Chinese sugar maker was brought to the islands—but his efforts could hardly be called successful. Desultory experiments continued for another half-century, while Hawaiian planters experimented with other crops, until Dr. Robert W. Wood bought the bankrupt mill of Ladd and Company—and made money out of it.

Soon there were mills all over the islands, with oxen or mules crushing the cane between wooden rollers—or sometimes with the use of water-power, where that was available. Then the juice was boiled, the molasses was drained away, and the crystallized sugar was hung up to dry. Very shortly the mills began to enlarge and modernize; better cane was imported from Tahiti; a newly-invented centrifugal machine separated the sugar from the molasses in a matter of minutes where the same process used to take weeks. Over seven thousand tons of sugar were exported in 1865. Then the huge irrigation projects were started that enabled thousands of acres of arid land to be used for cane. One seventeen-mile canal was built in 1876 by two sons of missionaries that was capable of carrying forty million gallons a day. Other entrepreneurs followed suit, and today a quarter of all American sugar is produced in Hawaii.

Incidentally, it was sugar also that brought the first Japanese immigrants to the islands—an occasion that was celebrated last year in Honolulu in the presence of Prince and Princess Hitachi.

HAWAII 🌺

"The first group of 153 Japanese immigrants," to quote Tokyo's *Japan Times*, "arrived in Honolulu June 19, 1868, aboard a British sailing ship to start a new life in Hawaii. The immigrants had left Yokohama 33 days before."

At that time King Kamehameha V sat on the island throne. Both he and his predecessor, Kamehameha IV, were grandsons of the great Kamehameha, and both of them ruled for only nine years.

Kamehameha IV, a bright and well-intentioned young man, ascended the throne when he was twenty years old. With his consort Emma, he established a court patterned after the English court of Queen Victoria, and the two Hawaiian monarchs followed the Victorian pattern also in their passion for "good works." The King hoped, during his reign, to free his kingdom from foreign bondage and to see the restoration of his people's health, which had been ravaged by imported disease.

But his reign was short and tragic. His heir, born in 1858, died after but four years, and the following year the King himself was dead. Queen Emma survived her royal husband for two decades, during which time she became a world-famous figure as well as one much loved by her people.

Kamehameha V also fought to free Hawaii from foreign domination, in particular that of the sugar planters, who kept demanding a reciprocity treaty with the United States so that their sugar might be imported free of duty. There was opposition in both America and Hawaii, and it was not until 1876 that the powerful planters got their way—through blackmail. Kamehameha V fought also against the importation of labor from China and Japan to work the plantations, but this fight he lost.

He did, however, succeed in promulgating a new Constitution, which he drew up himself in consultation with his Cabinet and the Supreme Court. Its aim was to increase the power of the throne, against the opposition of the foreigners, imposing a dictatorship on the country; but whatever real power the Hawaiian throne possessed may be said to have died with him in 1872—the fifth and last Kamehameha.

His successor, William C. Lunalilo, was elected to the kingship by an overwhelming majority over David Kalakaua, for Prince Lunalilo's popularity among the people was enormous. He was light-hearted and gay, intelligent and charming—but he was also a heavy drinker, and, though he was thirty-eight years old, he had not yet undergone the notoriously stabilizing influence of taking a wife. Ruling a country that desired to remain independent but whose most powerful residents were foreigners, with interests inimical to those of the majority, proved to be too much for him. His alcoholic intake increased alarmingly, and thirteen months after assuming the royal mantle he was dead of a lung disease.

He left his large personal estate to the poor of Hawaii and directed that his body be laid to rest, not in the Royal Mausoleum, but in Kawaiahao churchyard.

High Chief David Kalakaua, who succeeded him, was also thirty-eight when he was elected King on February 12, 1874, defeating Dowager Queen Emma. He was destined to reign for nearly two decades, and his reign was to prove almost as momentous in Hawaiian history as that of Kamehameha I, though unlike Kamehameha, Kalakaua was not the instigator of the events that made his reign so crucial.

That role was played by the flourishing sugar barons, who

31

supported Kalakaua's candidacy for the throne in return for his pledge to do all he could to secure the Reciprocity Treaty with the United States that the planters found so necessary. Throughout his reign, Kalakaua was torn between his own desire to rule a Hawaii that was essentially Hawaiian and the ever-growing power and greed of the foreign merchants. American almost to a man, the latter seemed to be interested more in increasing their already swollen bank accounts than in the welfare of the country that was supplying them with those vast sums of money.

This could not be said of the King. A high chief by descent, Kalakaua married High Chiefess Kapiolani, and together the monarchs did what they could to restore the waning health and prosperity of their people. The King believed that a rising birth rate would be one of the key solutions to the problem; the Queen apparently agreed with him, for she was later to bequeath her personal fortune to the foundation of a maternity home. The monarchs themselves were childless.

Two years after he ascended the throne, Kalakaua was in Washington, where, surrounded by his sugar-daddies (who had accompanied him officially as "advisers"), he was received by President Grant. The purpose of the meeting was, of course, to ram the Reciprocity Treaty home. There was, however, considerable opposition in the Senate, where it was claimed that the Treaty would be advantageous to the few great planters and distinctly disadvantageous to the people of Hawaii as a whole.

In reply, the planters suggested that unless the Treaty was approved, they would ship their sugar elsewhere—which would have meant the end both of American-Hawaiian trade and of American political influence in Hawaii. The Treaty was signed;

henceforward Hawaiian sugar was to enter the United States duty-free.

Kalakaua breathed a sigh—only in part of relief—and returned home. It was the same year—1876—that the two missionary sons completed construction of their seventeen-mile ditch that brought forty million gallons of water a day into the arid lowlands of Maui. Sugar cane, which is over seventy per cent liquid, thrives only where enormous amounts of water are available: some two thousand pounds of water are required for every pound of sugar.

Back in Hawaii, Kalakaua found himself increasingly wooed by and increasingly at odds with the foreigners, largely American, who by now owned most of Hawaii and who, not surprisingly, felt they had a right to interfere in her politics and government. Kalakaua was by nature a merry soul who enjoyed an evening's entertainment, which the foreign businessmen did their best to provide; they were also delighted to lend him money, for the King was an inveterate gambler. In return they wanted him to let them run the country, and they were able more and more to do so.

It is interesting to note that although Kalakaua was avowedly in favor of keeping Hawaii Hawaiian and of limiting immigration—chiefly of cheap labor from the East—the agreement to send Japanese workers to Hawaii was concluded while Kalakaua was on a state visit to Japan in 1881. At the same time he expressed the desire to see a Japanese imperial prince married to his niece, Princess Kaiulani, who was well up in the line of succession to the Hawaiian throne. This desire, however, was not destined to fulfillment.

The question of Japanese immigration was a thorny one—largely because, in accord with the established Imperial policy of total isolation, Japanese subjects not only were not encouraged, they were actually forbidden, to leave the country. When the first group of 153 emigrants—or, as some say, 150—left Yokohama in 1868, they did so at the orders of the Hawaiian consul and in defiance of the express prohibition of the Imperial government, which had just wrested control of Yokohama from the Tokugawa Shogunate.

The problem of future Japanese immigration into Hawaii was further complicated by the fact that many in this first group apparently felt that their working and living conditions in Hawaii had been misrepresented. Partly, of course, it was the fact that Japanese did not really like being anywhere but Japan, and partly it was the fact that working with sugar cane was far from easy or pleasant. But there can be no doubt that conditions on the large plantations were not utopian, and many Japanese complaints were justified. The monthly wage was four dollars, with free food, living quarters, and medical care; the workday started at around four in the morning and continued until nightfall. The complaints that reached Japan prompted the Imperial government to send a mission to Hawaii to look into the question. As a result, forty-two of the immigrants returned to Japan. When the three-year contract ended, twelve more went home, while forty left Hawaii for the American mainland, and there was no further Japanese immigration to Hawaii until after Kalakaua's visit.

Then, in 1885 a first group of 948 people, men and women, went to Hawaii under the new agreement, called, in Japan, the Kanyaku Imin (or "Government-arranged Emigration"). Between that year and 1894, twenty-seven groups of Japanese immigrants left for Hawaii, after which—until 1924—immigration was privately handled.

There was, it seemed, no end to the amount of labor the great plantations could absorb—but it had to be labor of a particular kind. It had to be laborers who had known extreme hardship and who were prepared to know more. The Japanese who came to Hawaii after 1885 were mostly from the drought- and famine-stricken areas of Honshu and Kyushu, where they had experienced actual starvation after several years of crop failure. In Hawaii they did not, at any rate, starve—however difficult and disagreeable the work was and however unpleasant the living conditions. The fervor that had inspired the missionaries half a century before appeared to have vanished: the Japanese set up the shrines they had brought with them and got down to work and little effort was made to christianize them.

Another group of people who had found working the sugar cane tolerable were Portuguese from Madeira and the Azores, who had also experienced extreme poverty and hardship in their native farms. Some twenty thousand of them came halfway across the world to Hawaii, where they settled down on the plantations and accepted the sometimes dreadful conditions. An attempt to import German and Norwegian farmers was not successful.

The monthly wage had by then risen to around twelve dollars for a man, eight for a woman; the workday was ten hours; the overseer carried a whip; failure to fulfill work standards entailed all sorts of onerous penalties; and the contract between worker and planter was unbreakable. Most Japanese apparently returned to the homeland after completion of their contract, though many stayed. They found other kinds of work and sent for their families or, if they had none, for their picture-brides. Their descendants now constitute about thirty per cent of the population of Hawaii.

HAWAII 🌱

King Kalakaua, on his return to Hawaii from his Asian tour, discovered that the foreign businessmen had tightened their grip on his government. When he dismissed a Cabinet member whom he considered too pro-American, he found the businessmen, with all their massive power, arrayed against him. Finally, in 1887, they forced him to accept a revision of the constitution which provided that legislators should henceforward be elected—and that only property-holders might vote. This latter provision effectively put the great landowners in control of the Hawaiian legislature.

Three years later, the planters received a serious setback, when the United States Congress passed the McKinley Tariff Bill, which removed the duty on all imported sugar and put a bounty of two cents a pound on domestic sugar. Horrified by this prospective decrease in revenue, the planters now decided that their best— indeed, their only—solution was to make Hawaiian sugar domestic. They began renewed agitation for annexation. Kalakaua himself was spared this battle: already ill, he went for medical treatment, in November, 1890, to San Francisco, where two months later he died.

It was his sister, and successor, Queen Liliuokalani, who was forced to fight. She had no choice—if she wanted to preserve her kingdom and fulfill what she believed to be her obligations both to herself and to her people. In an attempt, then, to combat foreign domination of her realm, she announced a "reformed" constitution that limited the franchise to Hawaiian subjects. It was a forlorn try—and one obviously doomed to failure. The Queen, ever since her accession, had been powerless: her Cabinet was largely American in composition, and it quite openly flouted her desires.

⚜ THE FIRST ALOHA STATE

At the promulgation of the "reforms," the planters took immediate action. An armed, underground "Committee for Safety" called on the American minister, who agreed to let marines from the *USS Boston* enter Hawaii, ostensibly to protect American property. January 16, 1893, was a night of unrest and fear; the following day, the Treasury was seized. With marines all over the city, the Queen felt she had no choice but to accede to the planters' demands and she advised her indignant subjects not to resist. She accordingly signed a statement consenting "to yield my authority until such time as the Government of the United States shall, upon the facts presented to it, undo the action of its representative and reinstate me in the authority which I claim as the constitutional sovereign of the Hawaiian Islands."

The revolutionists, having formed a "Provisional Government" under Judge Sanford Dole, sent a deputation to Washington to insist on annexation, while the American minister declared Hawaii an "American protectorate." But President Cleveland denounced the proposed Treaty of Annexation, saying, "To take the islands from the native people would be inconsistent with American honor, integrity and morality." The Secretary of State said, "I should oppose taking the islands by force and fraud." One orotund senator asked, "Is that day coming when along Pennsylvania Avenue we shall see a Hawaiian Queen, weighted down with sugar sacks on her back, pleading in behalf of her people for the right to institute a government for themselves?"

The President sent a special commissioner to Hawaii to investigate the details of the "revolution" and was horrified by the commissioner's report that it could not possibly have succeeded without the intervention of the American minister, since "the undoubted sentiment of the people is for the Queen. . . ." The President accordingly appointed a new minister, who brought word to the Queen that her throne would be restored to her if she would consent to grant amnesty to the members of the "Committee for Safety" and the "Provisional Government." Upon her acquiescence, the minister summoned the revolutionists to dissolve their illegal government. They refused. Challenging their own President, as they had the Queen of the country that had made them rich, they set up—on June 4, 1894—the Republic of Hawaii.

No official action was taken by the United States, so in January, 1895, the Hawaiians attempted a counter-revolution, which failed, and the Queen, along with hundreds of others, was tried for treason. Sentenced to twenty-five years at hard labor, she was imprisoned in a room at Iolani Palace, where she composed her famous, poignant *Aloha Oe*. She went to Washington on her release and was accorded a royal ovation, but by that time the fortunes of Hawaii were inextricably bound with those of the United States: on February 15, 1898, the battleship *Maine* was blown up in Havana; two months later the United States was at war with Spain; and on August 12 of that same year the Stars and Stripes replaced the flag of Hawaii over Iolani Palace. America, having realized the enormous strategic importance of the islands, as a result of the war, had made Hawaii a Territory of the United States. The war ended that same mid-August day.

Queen Liliuokalani lived on in retirement until 1917; on her death, she left her fortune to the orphans of her native land. Her niece, Princess Kaiulani, heiress-apparent to the Hawaiian throne, had been sent to London in May, 1889, to prepare to take up her duties as monarch of the islands. She was then fourteen years old—

"a delicate, exquisite beauty," as a Washington newspaper was to call her a few years later. Robert Louis Stevenson, when he was in Hawaii, wrote a poem on her departure:

> *From her land to mine she goes,*
> *The island maiden, the island rose—*
> *Light of heart and bright of face,*
> *This island daughter of a double race.*

Four years later, after her aunt, Queen Liliuokalani, had been overthrown, the young Princess journeyed to Washington, where she issued a proclamation which, although it was well received by the American people, was as unavailing as the efforts of her aunt and of the President of the United States. In 1897, she returned to Hawaii: on March 6, 1899, seven months after she had watched the Stars and Stripes raised over the palace she had thought was to be hers, she died. She was twenty-four years old. The history of Hawaii now becomes increasingly a part of the history of the great country that had annexed her and that, over half-a-century later, was to offer her the ultimate gift in its possession.

On annexation all citizens of Hawaii automatically became citizens of the United States. In 1900 the population of the islands was some 150,000—a mixture of peoples from all over the world who were to be governed now under the provisions of the Organic Act. The first of the Territory of Hawaii's twelve governors was Sanford B. Dole.

One of the earliest and most momentous acts in this new century of Hawaii's history was the abolition by Congress of the system of indentured labor. Thousands of those whom the Secretary of State had termed slaves "under another name" left the plantations, as soon as they heard the news, for Honolulu or their homeland or mainland America. Forty thousand Japanese went to California during those first five years. The planters had now to scour the world for other sources of "cheap, humble labor," which at that time they believed to be essential to sugar production.

Japan and the Philippines provided the chief sources of this labor—some three hundred thousand entered Hawaii before the passing of the Immigration Act in 1924. As the years wore on, the workers struck for increased wages—from five to seven cents an hour, from seventy-five cents to one dollar twenty-five a day. Nowadays, to be sure, the situation has drastically changed. Field workers on the great sugar plantations of Hawaii receive over twelve dollars a day, and their living conditions have improved beyond recognition. Much of this change must, of course, be attributed to the efforts, during and just after the war, of the I.L.W.U., which forced reform on the reluctant planters. After the war, the Big Five no longer "owned" the islands, and everything and everybody in them—but that change was still in the future; a lot remained to be done in Hawaii as the twentieth century moved shakily toward its half-way mark, bringing statehood to a territory.

"The Big Five" became a phrase as well known in the islands in the twentieth century as "The Kingdom of Heaven" had been in the nineteenth. The latter was probably easier to enter. At the height of their power, the Big Five not only controlled almost all of the islands' commerce but had extended their hegemony over banks, stores, insurance and trust companies, theaters and radio stations, and all the public utilities. Perhaps fifteen men in all ruled this vast empire, fifteen men who were intimately associated in their private as well as in their public lives and who saw eye-to-eye on all major matters of policy.

In the very beginning they were "factors," using a borrowed British term to denote that they were ready to supply whatever the sugar planters needed, in the way of materials or labor, to market the finished product, to ship it—in other words, to do whatever had to be done, to buy and sell whatever needed to be bought or sold. They also did the necessary bookkeeping, banking, and investing—as well as lending of money. Their hour of greatness may be said to have begun with the Reciprocity Treaty in 1876, and to have ended on December 7, 1941.

The oldest of the five is C. Brewer and Company, which goes back to a sea captain named James Hunnewell. He arrived in Hawaii in 1826 with some three thousand dollars worth of merchandise and opened a general store. The second oldest, Theo H. Davies & Co., the only British member of the Big Five, began in 1845 with an eighty-thousand dollar consignment of goods from Liverpool. The largest of the Five was founded in 1849 by a German sea captain, Henry Hackfeld; the vast assets of the company were seized during the First World War by the Alien Property Custodian, and the company—American Factors, Ltd.—went right on thriving. Castle and Cooke came into being in 1851, when two members of the missionary party of 1837 took over the stock that was left in the missionary commissary called the Depository. The last of the Big Five was established in 1894 by two sons of missionaries, Alexander and Baldwin.

In the decade following the Reciprocity Treaty, sugar production

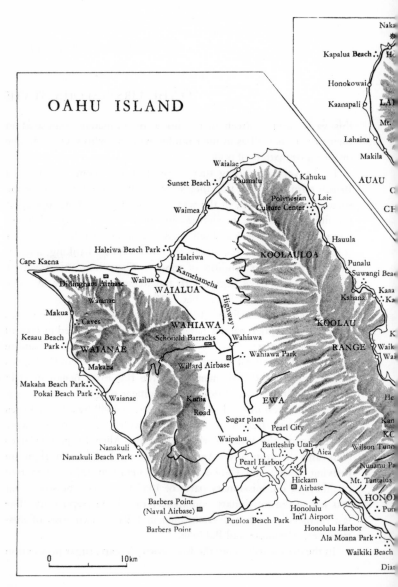

OAHU ISLAND

Naka

Kapalua Beach

Honokowai

Kaanapali · LÃ

Mt.

Lahaina

Makila

AUAU

Waialae

Sunset Beach · Paumalu   Kahuku

Polynesian · Laie
Culture Center

CH

Waimea

Hauula

Haleiwa Beach Park · ·   KOOLAULOA

Haleiwa   Punalu

Cape Kaena   Kamehameha   Suwangi Bea

Dillingham Airbase   Wailua   Kaaa · Ka

Waianae   WAIALUA   Kahana · · Ka

Makua   KOOLAU

· Caves   WAHIAWA

Keaau Beach   Schofield Barracks   Wahiawa   RANGE   Waik
Park · ·   WAIANAE   · · Wahiawa Park   Wai

Makaha   Willard Airbase

Makaha Beach Park · ·   Kunia
Pokai Beach Park · ·   Waianae   Road   EWA   He

Sugar plant   Kan

Pearl City   KC

Nanakuli   Waipahu   Battleship Utah   Wilson Tun

Nanakuli Beach Park · ·   Aiea   Nuuanu P

Pearl Harbor   Mt. Tantalus

Hickam   HONO
Barbers Point   Airbase   · Pur
(Naval Airbase)   Honolulu
Int'l Airport

Barbers Point   Puuloa Beach Park   Honolulu Harbor
Ala Moana Park · ·

Waikiki Beach

Dia

0   10km

42

MAUI ISLAND

Kahakuloa

Waihea

Pauwela

Kahului Airport

Paia

Kailua

Wailuku
Valley
Museum

Kahului

Kaumahina Park

Puunene

Makawao

Keanae

Wailua

Waikapu

WAILUKU

Black Sand
Beach

Hana Airport

Maalaea

MAKAWAO

Huakoa Park

Kaeleku

Hana Bay Park

Kihei

Waiakoa

Mt. Hanakauhi
2713

Hana

Kalama Park

Observatory

Haleakala National Park

HANA

Keawakapu

Red Hill
3055

Haleakala Crater

St. Mary Statue

Hamoa
Beach

Kula Sanatorium

Makena

Heiau

Kipahulu

Seven

ALALAKEIKI

Kaupo

Sacred Lakes

CHANNEL

Mokulau

ALENUIHAHA

Makapuu
Point

CHANNEL

Makapuu
Peninsula

Kailua Bay

Kalama

Kailua Beach Park

Lanikai

0   10km

Mt. Olomana

Waimanalo

Waimanalo Beach Park

Kaiona Beach Park

Seal Park

Makapuu Beach
Park

Kuliowaowa

Wawamalu Beach
Park

Koko Head
Natural Park

Hanauma Bay Beach Park

increased prodigiously, and so did the profits of the factors who were supplying labor and equipment and who were looking after sales and distribution. With the McKinley Tariff Bill, in 1890, many of the smaller plantations were forced out of business; the factors stood ready to buy. They were soon powerful enough to accomplish the dethronement of Queen Liliuokalani; although they can hardly be said to have arranged for the Spanish-American War, they certainly profited by the annexation that followed it.

During the first three decades of the new century, there appeared to be no check to their ever-growing power—but with the thirties, it became obvious that the time of absolutism was ending. The Big Five were challenged both by their own labor and by competition from the mainland. To check the rising agitation in favor of unions, they voluntarily raised wages, improved living conditions, and supplied workers with medical care and hospitalization. Workers replied that they did not want the feudal paternalism of the Big Five, they wanted the right to organize into their own unions, controlled by themselves, and to bargain collectively with their employers. In 1940, the National Labor Relations Board held an election, as a result of which the winning union signed a contract for the workers with the company: an unprecedented event in the history of Hawaiian sugar. At the same time that they were being threatened by labor, the Big Five were being threatened by capital. Several large mainland companies—against severe opposition— were able to find sites and open stores, and for the first time the people of Hawaii could experience the thrilling delight of shopping at competitive prices.

A third threat to the autocracy of the Big Five was the emergence of the new middle class, children of the immigrants as well as of native Hawaiians, who had been to school, who had even been to a university. Of mixed parentage—Japanese and Chinese, Portuguese and Filipino, Puerto Rican and Hawaiian, they were native-born Americans, and they were no more prepared than other native-born Americans anywhere to accept conditions so at variance with their rights and guarantees. One of the things they began to do was agitate for the election of legislators who did not represent the Big Five.

Then, at 7:59 a.m., December 7, 1941, Japanese dive bombers attacked the airfield on Ford Island, in the center of Pearl Harbor, and a few seconds later the vessels in "battleship row" nearby: it was the beginning of a new and tragic and sometimes glorious chapter in Hawaiian history. The United States had had the "exclusive right to enter the harbor of Pearl River" since 1887; in April, 1940, Rear Admiral Joseph Taussig told the Senate that "war with Japan is inevitable"; the Honolulu *Advertiser* for November 30, 1941, printed a story under the banner head: JAPANESE MAY STRIKE OVER WEEKEND; and by that time the Army and Navy had spent three-quarters of a billion dollars to make Pearl Harbor impregnable to enemy attack—which, in one-quarter of an hour, in the worst defeat the United States had ever known, rendered the impregnable fortress powerless.

Hawaii was at war, and like everywhere else in the world would never be the same again once the war was over. For one thing, the Big Five would never again experience the thrill of absolute autocracy: much of their power, like much of their commerce, went by the board. Hawaii became headquarters for the Pacific War, and conducting the war naturally took precedence over every other consideration.

A few hours after the attack, the governor of the Territory of Hawaii invoked the wide emergency powers that had been invested in him in case of necessity, but he was never to make use of them, for the commander of the Army in Hawaii, General Walter C. Short, called on the governor demanding that martial law be declared and all authority be ceded to the Army. One of the reasons Short gave for this extraordinary demand was the large number of Japanese who inhabited the islands; and the governor, after some hesitation, agreed. He not only delegated his own powers as governor but also those "normally exercised by judicial officers and employees of this territory." The authority of both the United States and the Big Five had been replaced by that of the Army—in what has been called the most amazing military *coup d'état* in American history.

The islands were now under martial law, and the three powers that Americans had so painfully separated—executive, legislative, and judicial—were now held by one man, the military governor. He issued his commands in the form of general orders, which covered every aspect of the islanders' life. It is perhaps as great a tribute as any to the people who lived in Hawaii that in the interest of winning the war they accepted a situation that most Americans would have found intolerable.

The face of Hawaii was, of course, utterly changed during the war. Hundreds of thousands of tourists became hundreds of thousands of men in uniform, beaches were covered with barbed wire, and camouflage was hopefully painted over prominent buildings.

The planters, before the war, had consistently refused to grow food-stuffs instead of sugar; Hawaii therefore had been dependent on the mainland for most of its food; and so with the declaration of war came critical shortages, which, although they eased off, never entirely disappeared. In the last year of the Pacific War, a thousand soldiers a day passed through Hawaii.

A presidential proclamation ended martial law on October 24, 1944, and after the war was over, the United States Supreme Court repudiated the Army's *coup d'état*. And after the war was over, Americans everywhere discovered that the 442nd Regimental Combat Team, composed of Japanese-Americans from both the mainland and Hawaii, had won over six thousand decorations, to become the most decorated unit in United States Army history, while the Japanese-American 100th Infantry Battalion was nick-named "the Purple Heart Battalion." When the War Department had, at one point, called for fifteen hundred more volunteers from among Hawaii's Japanese population, over ninety-five hun-dred applied! Of Hawaii's war dead, eighty per cent were of Japanese ancestry.

Professor Thomas D. Murphy, of the Department of History of the University of Hawaii, has described the difficult and sometimes painful return to their native islands of those Japanese Hawaiians who survived. "It was easy enough," he writes, of the agitation and anguish that attended the end of the war in Japan, "to tell those of Japanese ancestry to maintain a calm and broad outlook, but it was sometimes difficult for AJA [Americans of Japanese Ancestry] veterans to maintain it, when they encountered criticism that they had returned home with too 'cocky' an attitude. Charlie Hemenway exasperatedly commented that those who made the charge had had, before the war, a concept of the Nisei* as a lesser breed of second-class status who were supposed to be properly respectful, submissive, and grateful for all small favors. Now that these boys had come home from the war with a greater degree of self-assurance and a feeling that they had earned first-class citizenship, some of the island people still persisted in treating them as inferiors. The veterans naturally refused to take it, and they were called 'cocky.' "

Professor Murphy continues, a little later: "Many islanders who had never been hostile to the AJA's had found themselves annoyed at the amount of print devoted to the deeds of the 100th and the 442nd. . . . It was easy, now that the Nisei had proved themselves, to forget what things had been like for these young men from 1939 through 1943. It was also easy for some islanders to forget—and for others perhaps difficult to realize—that the achievement of the 100th, the 442nd, and the AJA interpreters was not simply a Hawaiian story, but one which had implications for the whole of the nation. Men of good will, sitting at typewriters in the War Department and in other governmental agencies, in newspaper offices, behind magazine desks, and elsewhere saw the story of the Nisei servicemen from the islands as an American saga. They wanted the contrast between Hawaii's spirit of *aloha* and California's intolerance—and the wartime results which had stemmed from each—to be known to as many Americans as possible. Harry Truman had succinctly expressed this viewpoint when he had reviewed five hundred veterans of the 442nd at the White House. 'You fought not only the enemy but you fought prejudice—and you have won.

---

*Children of Japanese immigrants, born under the American flag.

Keep up that fight and we will continue to win—to make this great republic stand for just what the Constitution says it stands for—the welfare of all of the people all of the time. Bring forward the colors.' "*

It may even be questioned whether Hawaii would have succeeded in achieving the statehood she so ardently desired but for the remarkable achievements of these Nisei volunteers. Statehood had long been a Hawaiian dream—but, for some reason, no more than a dream. After the war there seemed to be more cause than ever for that dream to become reality, but still it failed to do so.

In 1946 President Truman demanded "that Congress promptly accede to the wishes of the people of Hawaii that the Territory be admitted to statehood in our union," and a year later the House of Representatives approved. But the Senate held back. Whether it was because of the "sugar-state" senators, or—as some said—the "white-supremacy state" senators, or—as still others suggested—the senators who were in the pocket of the United States Navy, or whether it was due to the efforts of the Big Five themselves, the fact remains that for fourteen years after the war's end Hawaii continued to be a territory. Then finally, in March, 1959, both the Senate and the House passed the Statehood Bill. Dream had at last become reality.

Now tourists from forty-nine sister states may go to Hawaii to see at least one aspect of democracy in action: total racial equality. Hawaii points out that one reason for this happy situation is its mixed ancestral background and the difficulty of disentangling the

---

*Thomas D. Murphy, *Ambassadors in Arms* (Honolulu: University of Hawaii Press, 1954).

mixture and separating the various strains. Hawaiians of mainly Japanese ancestry at present number over two hundred thousand, and so do Caucasians of mainly American or European ancestry; there are more than sixty thousand who claim descent from Filipinos, more than thirty thousand from Chinese, ten thousand Puerto Ricans, seven thousand Koreans, and three thousand Negroes. But the terms are inaccurate (and so, very likely, are the figures), for these are all Americans, many of whom have intermarried, as have some seventy-five thousand Hawaiians who are partly or largely native Polynesian. Twelve thousand pure Hawaiians still live on islands that once were theirs alone.

A number of minor factors may contribute to the single major fact that people on the islands do live in peace and brotherhood, unworried about the race-riots that torment Hawaii's sister-states: it may be the easy climate, or the new prosperity, or the fact that Oriental peoples—if they were not tolerant by nature—have learned how to be tolerant, some of them the hard way.

Or is it the fact that Hawaii is a land where *aloha* is still a word in common use? Daniel K. Inouye, the Hawaiian Nisei who is now a United States senator, says:

"When I was in the Army I had friends who were both black and white, and I often acted as a successful intermediary between them. A man who has learnt to greet another with honest affection is not apt to cut the other's throat—or even deny him his rights.

"Isn't this role the very one Hawaii can play for her own country —and the world—in the future?"

◄5. *Of pure-blooded Hawaiians,* only about twelve thousand have survived the various waves of immigration; the resulting mixture, however, is seldom unbeautiful.

6. *At Kodak Hawaii* show, in Kapi lani Park, hula dancers prepare to "on-stage," the stage being a law In the background sits an actor rep senting Kamehameha the Great.

7. *Dancers* can express anything from man's earliest reverence for the gods to the pounding of taro root to make *poi*, which is what the man at the left is representing. In former days, men did all the cooking, and many foods were tabu for women.

8. *Tourists* watching a hula performance: dark glasses, muumuus (those flowery Hawaiian "nightgowns"), aloha shirts, and hats made of coconut leaves combine to create a distinctively Hawaiian picture.

9. *Comic hula* may well be as old in Hawaiian history as sacred hula. Hawaiian girls, as they grow older, are likely to put on weight—but in the islands this is not thought to detract from their beauty.

10. *White sand* (*see previous page*) of Waikiki must be constantly replenished with sand brought from other beaches, since Waikiki itself is narrow and its waves are not always pacific.

11. *Queen's Surf* Barefoot Bar is famous for its Hawaiian band—as well as for one of the best male hula dancers in the islands.

12. *Luau,* with whole pig steamed in an underground oven, is the classic Hawaiian feast. Diners usually sit on the ground—but this *luau* was arranged especially for tourists.

13. *Hula lessons* are given even at night on Waikiki Beach—and usually everyone has a try at it, regardless of age, sex, or shape.

14. *Leis (see previous page)* are one way Hawaiians express their pleasure at welcoming visitors. These stalls, in front of Honolulu Airport, sell leis ranging in price from one dollar to ten.

15. *Network of highways* crisscrosses Oahu; cars move more slowly than on the mainland, and there are few large trucks.

17. *Breakwater* at Waikiki Beach allows for placid bathing; surfriders go out beyond the breakwater, where the waves sometimes rise to stupendous heights.

◀16. *Aloha Tower* (*see previous page*), 184 feet high, chimes out "Aloha Oe" and provides a fine view, from the tenth floor, of Honolulu and the harbor. State and national flags fly side-by-side.

18. *Getting a tan* is one of the ▶ chief objects of Hawaii's visitors—and most of them use these *goza* (grass mats) made in Japan and sold in every shop on the beach.

19. *Hotels in the* background, lifeguard in the center, and people everywhere: it's hard to believe that sixty years ago Waikiki was an almost deserted marshland.

20. *Hawaiian youths* who work as lifeguards and teach surfing are—quite obviously—attractive to the tourists. Romance in Hawaii blossoms as effortlessly as the orchids.

21. *Diversity* of beaches in the islands ▶ permits surfing the year around at one place or another. Some, with huge breakers and tricky currents, are extremely dangerous.

22. *Canoeing,* another traditional Hawaiian sport, was revived in 1908 by Alexander Hume Ford, who formed the Outrigger Canoe Club, whose beach house was the beginning of Waikiki.

23. *Ala Wai* Boat Harbor, near Waikiki, headquarters for two yacht clubs, can berth over five hundred craft.

24. *Sea Life Park,* at Makapuu Beach (about half an hour by car from Waikiki), has one of the world's most comprehensive exhibits of marine life, and its trained dolphins at Whalers Cove are the best educated in the world.

25. *Hanauma Bay,* below Koko Head, at the southern tip of Oahu, is a public park with a glorious beach less crowded than the beaches nearer Honolulu; coral reefs are clearly visible through the transparent water.

26. *Wood carving* from the Heiau Holo-Holo-Ku, the oldest *heiau* (or place of worship) on the island of Kauai, which is said to be where the first Polynesians landed a millennium ago. Ku was the dread god of war, one of whose perquisites was regular human sacrifice. The images seen here in this restored *heiau* are copies—the originals are in the Bishop Museum in Honolulu.

27. *Outside the heiau* stand the royal birthstones where the *alii* of Hawaii retired to give birth to their royal children, whose umbilical cords were preserved there. The precincts were tabu to commoners; infringement of the tabu meant death.

28. *Monument* to Captain Cook, who
"discovered" the islands in 1778 and
was killed the following year at a
point not far from here; the monument was erected in 1874.

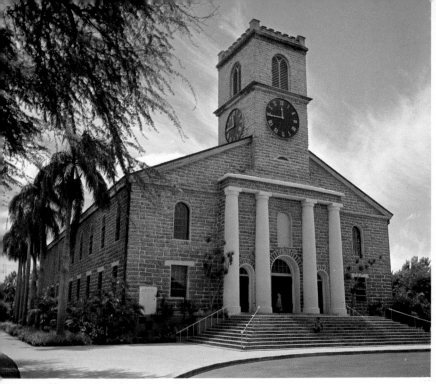

29. *Kawaihao Church,* oldest in Honolulu, was built in 1842.

31. *Lyman House* Memorial Museum, on Hawaii, built in 1839, reconstructed in 1854.

THE FIRST HAWAIIAN CHRISTIAN,
HENRY OPUKAHAIA,
DIED AT CORNWALL, CONN. 1818

THE FIRST CHRISTIAN
MISSIONARIES TO HAWAII
BINGHAM, THURSTON, WHITNEY,
LANDED AT KAILUA, APRIL 12, 1820
WITH THEIR HAWAIIAN COMRADES
HOPU, KANUI, HONOLII.

30. *Memorial* to Henry Opukahaia, whose conversion and death inspired the missionaries.

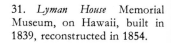

LYMAN HOME
REMODELLED
IN
1854

32. *Gilded   bronze*
statue of Kameha-
meha I in Honolulu
is decorated with leis
on June 11, Kameha-
meha Day.

33. *Royal   navy—*
engraved on pedestal
of statue—that Kame-
hameha used to unify
the islands.

34. *Nuuanu Valley* (*see previous page*) where King Kamehameha defeated the forces of King Kalanikupule of Oahu.

37. *Iolani Palace,* the only royal palace on American territory and now the seat of the Hawaii State Legislature.

36. *Princess Kaiulani,* niece of Queen Liliuokalani, who went to Washington in an attempt to preserve the monarchy she was intended to rule.

35. *Throne* of Hawaiian monarchs, preserved in Iolani Palace.

38. *Pearl Harbor.*

39. *Arizona Memorial,* where the names of the officers and men who went down with the battleship are inscribed.

40. *Utah,* half-submerged, was one of the casualties of the Japanese attack of December 7, 1941.

41. *National Memorial Cemetery* of the Pacific, in Punchbowl Crater, contains the graves of nineteen thousand men who died in the Second World War and the Korean War.

42. *Memorial* honoring the 442nd Regimental Combat Team, composed of Americans of Japanese ancestry from both the mainland and Hawaii—the most decorated unit in United States Army history.

43. *Sugar cane* being harvested by machinery, one of the many modern improvements in the formerly back-breaking work of turning cane into sugar. A Hawaiian industry that, it was thought, could not exist without the equivalent of slave labor is now more highly mechanized than sugar plantations anywhere and pays the world's highest wages for field-workers.

44. *Dole* Hawaiian Pineapple Company, in Honolulu, claims it is the world's largest fruit cannery, with machinery that can process a million pineapples every four hours. During the busy summer months, some three hundred million cans of pineapple are produced by this company alone —about forty per cent of Hawaii's total.

45. *Pineapple fields* are terraced, to combat soil erosion, and during the season, harvesting is done, both day and night, by these huge mechanical boom harvesters equipped with spotlights. Dole's largest field is on the island of Lanai.

46. *Papaya* is a popular food in Hawaii as in all semi-tropical countries; far richer than oranges in both vitamins A and C, it is commonly eaten for breakfast with a little lemon juice squeezed over it.

47. *Bananas* grow in almost endless variety—long, short, green, and yellow; Honolulu's supermarkets provide a good place to see and sample the many types.

48. *Mango* is thought by many Hawaiians to be the finest fruit of all—and many non-Hawaiians agree.

93

49. *Coffee* is grown mainly in the Kona District of the island of Hawaii by small Japanese farmers; work is hard, and profits are slight.

50. *Souvenirs* for the tourists keep many a Hawaiian gainfully employed; the total annual number of visitors to the islands now exceeds that of its residents.

51. *Orchids* are widely cultivated; here a girl sorts blooms at the Oda Orchid Farm in Hilo.

52. *Anthurium* (below left), which stays fresh for a long time after cutting, is much used by Japanese for flower-arranging.

53. *Plumeria* (called frangipani elsewhere and *melia* in Hawaiian) is one of the most popular flowers for the making of leis.

54. *Shower tree*: this one is gold, other colors being pink and coral.

56. *Hibiscus*, the state flower, is most popular of all; it seems to grow everywhere and boasts over five thousand varieties, some botanists say, on the islands.

55. *Bird of Paradise* may be orange-and-blue (as above) or white.

57. *Two American women* wearing muumuus typify the conglomerate nature of Hawaiian society, where people of the most varied ethnic background —from Madeira to Korea—live harmoniously together and where racial tension is virtually unknown. The muumuu is a modern adaptation of the Mother Hubbard with which the missionaries clothed the ample nakedness of the Hawaiian ladies they encountered on their arrival. It is now almost the "national dress" of female Hawaii and will be seen always and everywhere—from classes in the University to formal parties.

58.   *Inter-island* travel is in the hands of two airlines, there being no regularly scheduled passenger ships. Informally dressed, barefoot passengers are a common sight on board the planes.

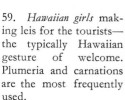

59.   *Hawaiian girls* making leis for the tourists— the typically Hawaiian gesture of welcome. Plumeria and carnations are the most frequently used.

60. *Hawaiian life* is free and easy, the weather is superb, and there are plenty of places for an informal alfresco picnic.

61. *Holoku* is patterned, like the muumuu, after the New England Mother Hubbard—difference is that the *holoku* has a slightly tighter waist and a longer skirt.

62. *A typical* middle-class Hawaiian home—and whatever the work, cars are a necessity in daily life.

63. *Hawaiians,* said Mark Twain, "are fonder of theology than they are of pie." Honolulu's churches are Catholic, Protestant, and Jewish as well as Buddhist.

64. *"Issei"* is the Japanese word for first-generation immigrants, those born in Japan; their children are "Nisei." Japanese first came to Hawaii in 1868, and now play an important role in the islands' economy and administration.

65. *Japanese* have a word for everything: here *Nisei* and *Sansei* (third-generation immigrants) enjoy a Japanese barbecue on their picnic and play *hanafuda,* a card-game imported from the homeland.

66. *Hawaii Times* is the largest Japanese-language newpaper on the islands; shown at right is its composing-room.

67. *Hawaii's* Japanese, unlike those of the mainland, almost all know something of their ancestral language; here is a school for *Yonsei* (fourth-generation immigrants).

68. *Recordings* of songs by Japanese singers are all the rage. Amateur singing contests in the Japanese language are held by local radio and television stations weekly.

◀69. *Notoriously hard-working,* like their counterparts at home, are the Americans of Japanese ancestry on Hawaii; they play just as hard (*see previous page*).

71. *Bon odori*—Japanese dances to honor the dead—are held every weekend throughout the summer in Hawaii, where they are even more popular than in Japan.

70. *Buddhist temple* of the Sōtō sect is one of twenty-two in Honolulu; there are over a hundred Buddhist temples in all of Hawaii.

72. *Diamond Head,* the awe-inspiring, world-famous background to the capital's many skyscrapers, got its name when some English seafarers picked up a handful of volcanic crystals they thought were diamonds. An extinct volcano, Diamond Head was once the home of the goddess Pele.

113

74. *Students* at the University reflect the diversity of ethnic backgrounds of the islands' population; seven queens are elected annually at the spring beauty contest.

73. *University of Hawaii* has special courses in oceanography and typhoons, fruit flies and diseases of the pineapple, anthropology and Oriental culture.

75. *East-West Center*—more accurately, the Center for Cultural and Technical Exchange between East and West—is supported by the Government and every year invites guest lecturers from all over Asia.

76. *Residential section* of Honolulu, of which there are many now that the population has leapt to over three hundred thousand. Yet the city's housing shortage remains acute.

77. *Ala Moana Center,* in central Honolulu, has all sorts of stores and restaurants as well as fountains and sculptures, a Japanese garden and a replica of Peking's Summer Palace gate. On top, the revolving restaurant makes one complete turn every hour.

78. *Escalators* at the Center are forbidden—the signs say so—to barefooted people; but not everybody reads signs.

Inside the Center are shops of almost every persuasion, including a super-deluxe food market, a Sears-Roebuck, and a Japanese department store called Shirokiya.

80. *Liliuokalani Park,* one of the sights on the island of Hawaii. Hawaii is the biggest island in the archipelago, some nine times larger in area than Oahu, where the capital, Honolulu, is located. The population, however, is only about a tenth that of Oahu. Nevertheless, it is known as "the big island" and contains the biggest ranch in the world, Hawaii's famous Parker Ranch. It saw the birth of Kamehameha the Great and the death of Captain Cook.

81. *Hilo*, the capital of the island of
Hawaii, is connected with Honolulu
by commuter planes, which take just
over an hour; above is a not uncom-
mon scene at Hilo's airport.

82. *Hukilau Hotel* in Hilo, second largest city in the islands, is famous for its Hawaiian cuisine.

83. *Sampan* is Hilo's answer to the transportation problem: it carries twelve passengers.

84. *Akaka Falls* (*see previous page*) drop 420 feet into Kolekole Stream —all in a sixty-six acre, richly verdant state park where visitors may picnic amid the cool and quiet green.

85. *Kalapana Beach,* bordered by palm trees, is made up of lava from Kilauea that burst into fragments as it hit the water; the constant action of the waves keeps grinding the lava finer and finer.

124

86. *Kilauea,* the largest active volcano in Hawaii, is part of Hawaii Volcanoes National Park, which was established to preserve one of the world's most remarkable volcanic areas.

87. *Lava tunnel* of Kilauea, 450 feet long, was formed when the outer crust hardened while the molten lava within continued its onward flow; Fern Jungle is famous.

88. *Halemaumau,* the largest and most active lava vent in Kilauea Crater, has a diameter of three thousand feet; its depth changes, of course, as the bottom collapses or refills.

89. *Fern Jungle,* in the Hawaii Volcanoes National Park, is a cool forest of giant tree ferns of numerous species as well as a number of smaller varieties.

129

90. *Kailua-Kona,* in the Kona District of Hawaii, is a world-famous center for deep-sea fishing; it also has a number of hotels and restaurants, and life is friendly and informal.

91. *Monument* to Prince Kuhio, who was born in the island of Kauai in 1871 and who for long years represented Hawaii in the United States Congress after the abolition of the monarchy. Kauai is thought to be the first of the islands to have been inhabited by the adventuring Polynesians and its Heiau Holo-Holo-Ku (Plates 26 and 27) is the oldest extant place of worship in all Hawaii. Because of the richness of its flora, Kauai is called the Garden Island—an epithet it thoroughly deserves.

92. *Nawiliwili Harbor* is Kauai's chief port, but it is also a resort, with a fine, well-protected beach, hotels and restaurants.

93. *Hotel* in Kauai consists of cottages set amid the rich green; names of many hotels in Kauai begin with the word *hale,* which means "house" in Hawaiian.

94. *Hulas* are performed nightly in many of Kauai's hotel bars; if dances are not altogether authentic, visitors seem to enjoy them just the same.

95. *Waimea Canyon* State Park, in the western part of Kauai, has been called the Little Grand Canyon—and it is easy to see why.

96. *At Haena,* in Kauai, there are two "wet caves" which legend says were dug by Pele, the fire goddess, in search of a dwelling-place. ▶

97. *Coco Palms Hotel,* in the midst of a thirty-two-acre palm grove, at the mouth of the Wailua River, that used to belong to the royal family of Kauai, is famous for its combination of luxury and simplicity.

98. *Replica* of missionaries' grass-roofed church stands in hotel grounds.

99. *Excursion boats* go up Wailua River to Fern Grotto, passing the royal burial grounds. First Polynesians are said to have settled at the river's mouth.

100. *Songs* accompany the visitors as they head up-river, and the captains of the boats retell legends associated with the region.

101. *Fern Grotto,* one of the best-known sights on the island, is a damp cave with a jungle of luxuriant ferns. After the guide has finished her explanation, the tourists will be serenaded by a chorus from inside the grotto, which is famous for its acoustics.

102. *Iao Valley* is one of the most spectacular sights on the island of Maui. Shown below, to the left, is the famous volcanic monolith called Iao Needle, which soars almost straight up to a height of 2,250 feet. Maui is the second largest of the Hawaiian group of islands and the third in population. It is forty-five minutes by air from Honolulu and is named after the god who not only brought the islands up from the bottom of the sea but also gave its inhabitants the gift of fire.

103. *Kula,* at a height of three thousand feet above sea level, is the chief center of Maui's floriculture. Shown above are descendants of Japanese immigrants who have settled here—the flowers they are picking will probably be flown to Honolulu and drape the necks of tomorrow's tourists.

104. *Hana*, on Maui's eastern shore, was cut off from the rest of the island until the road was built in 1927 and so retains much of its original Polynesian charm; most of its inhabitants are pure or part Hawaiian. Shown below is one of the "Seven Sacred Lakes," which were once tabu for commoners.

105. *Haleakala,* the world's largest dormant volcanic crater, means "House of the Sun," and it was here, according to legend, that the god Maui imprisoned the sun to make the day longer and so give man more time for fishing.

106. *Silver Sword,* with its sword-shaped silver leaves and its stalk, several feet high, bearing a profusion of small, chrysanthemum-like flowers.

107. *Banyan Tree* was brought to Lahaina in 1873 from India, where it is considered sacred.

108. *Lahaina,* once a great whaling center, still preserves some of the cannon that once guarded it in its days of greatness.

109. *Father Damien,* the Belgian priest who did so much to alleviate the lot of the lepers exiled to the island of Molokai; he himself was stricken with the disease and died of it there. The disease can now be cured, and the dreadful conditions that prevailed on Molokai are a nightmare of the past. The two other inhabited islands of the archipelago are privately owned, Lanai by the Dole Hawaiian Pineapple Company Ltd., and Niihau by the Robinson family. The latter, a seventy-three-square-mile rock, on which live some two hundred pure-blooded Hawaiians, is closed to all visitors save those invited by the residents themselves or by the Robinsons. It is what Hawaii used to be—and so long as it continues to be *kapu* will probably remain so.

110.   The sun sets on a Hawaiian beach.

THIS BEAUTIFUL WORLD